IN ABSOLUTES
WE SEEK EACH OTHER

JESSICA JOHNSON

IN ABSOLUTES
WE SEEK EACH OTHER

JESSICA JOHNSON

NEW MICHIGAN PRESS
TUCSON, ARIZONA

NEW MICHIGAN PRESS
DEPT OF ENGLISH, P. O. BOX 210067
UNIVERSITY OF ARIZONA
TUCSON, AZ 85721-0067

<http://newmichiganpress.com/nmp>

Orders and queries to nmp@thediagram.com.

Copyright © 2014 by Jessica Johnson.
All rights reserved.

ISBN 978-1-934832-44-8. FIRST PRINTING.

Printed in the United States of America.

Design by Ander Monson.

Cover image © Gorshkov13 | Dreamstime.com - Developing Fish Eggs Photo

CONTENTS

I. A DIFFERENCE IN THE FIELD

"A greenhouse ceiling opens on its gears"   3
Greenhouse   4
"At first, strange things seemed possible"   5
Artifacts   6
Individuals   8
Pool   9
Jellyfish   10
Individuals   11
Indoctrination   13
In Absolutes We Seek Each Other   15
Hatchery   16
Bodies in Motion   18
The Isolate   19
Possessions   20
In Situ   21
Gels   23
"Here is what happens: the lab coat"   24
Pool   25
Search Engine   26
"A population flows"   28

2. COORDINATES

Driving North   31
Barnacles   32
Anatomy   33
Savants   34
Apertures   35
Blood Harmony   36
Moon Snail   37
Anatomy   38
Coordinates   39
Teleology of Islands   41
White   42
Anatomy   43
Aubade   44
Arc & Chord   45
Meanwhile   46
Prologue   47

Acknowledgments   48

I

A DIFFERENCE IN THE FIELD

¤

The greenhouse ceiling opens on its gears:
a season out of season.
Breathing plants enrich the air.
In a glass house, revelation.

I am only eye and ear.
No one here will know me.
The wall of panes, milked up, repaints
a tour group as shapes, cascading.

What is a ghost but memory, a net
un-bodied, sweeping through a place?
Passing through a bit of past to see
what catches in the throat.

GREENHOUSE

The boss, P, walked me through the exhibitions
on the day I started work, past vines
and massive ferns: a gallery of forms.

In the tropical room, each shape overgrew
the next; we crossed sweet spots in the air, she
pointed out vanilla pods, an orchid's fruit.
P cared for what she could explain:
how vanilla flavor can be made from pine,
how the gourd vines coevolved with humankind,
how the corpse plant draws a beetle
with the reek of rotting flesh,
the advantageous angle of a certain stem
the potential in a trough of brew: blue-green
algae, which she called the next big thing.

None were wonders, no matter how strange,
none were beauties, no color or line
enchanted P, none held her own
unknowns, none existed for its own sake.
The traits we saw or could not see were answers
to our questions, were tools to meet our
purpose. There was nothing wild
in the jungle made of glass.

¤

At first, strange things seemed possible. We dropped
microscopic seeds on dirt; they grew; we staked
the seedlings straight; they lived on light.

We listed to slack-key guitar and lost ourselves in work.
The silver-painted pipes oozed canopies of mist; the ceiling turned;
a long note finished the guitar's phrase, veered from flat to sharp,

pulling us toward a tropic July, in the middle
of a northern winter. Soon our seedling (wild-type at first)
filled every table: Arabidopsis thaliana, mouse-eared cress, a
mustard weed you've

seen in the backyard or roadside ditch. Each with the same
ruffled mouse-eared leaves, same crisp stems, same optimistic
pose, leaves tenderly displayed to the overhead light.

Clones, they were made to show a difference in the field,
should one arise: pale leaves, short stem, golden seed, early growth,
sterility, long limbs, a technician bending to reach them,

smooth arms standing out against a field of green.

ARTIFACTS

We found a frozen timepiece dangling from
the cabinet knob. Martin's, maybe. He was born
there in 1910—the slant, converted house we had the upstairs
of. His hand almost too shaky to sign the lease when M
and I moved in. The kitchen used to be a child's room.
A pastel balloon-scape showed through layers of cheap paint.

The house told time, in its way.
The framework gave to gravity;
the tilt grew more pronounced. The bathtub
had a shallow end. Cakes turned out wedge-shaped.
We watched the street through rippling windows
and the tracks of dirty rain.

Martin shuffled over once a week to mow the lawn
and tweak the wiring, as bulb after bulb flickered out.
He pulled the tangled wires down and claimed
to know their logic. In disarray the house held
up as sparks flew through the circus in the ceiling
while we slept. The house resisted sunlight, too, that rose across
the floorboards scuffed past fading,
and slant-wise ebbed.
It came, moved through,
and never left a mark.

That day we wound the watch, it ticked a day or two,
then stopped. We thought we'd paint the place
to make it ours (a blue in M's room she called Sleep,
my room a greenish slate), pass through the warped box
cleanly, then on to better things. In fact we'd leave
our artifacts—grease splatters on the wall
beside the antique stove, hair on the linoleum.
We had no way of knowing how our story
would be told: the duct tape where we'd try
to patch the pipes, our walking-patterns on the floor.

INDIVIDUALS

The idea was to mess them up, our plants,
bombard our slate-clean seeds with agents
that would slightly tweak their DNA, then plant
the seeds, and let them grow into a bank of freaks.

(It came to pass. We saw, in the boss's terms,
a panoply of fucked-upness. Spindly maidens,
broad-leafed giants, dwarves in
a blizzard of twisted flowers.)

With sterile scissors,
we snipped a teense from each,
and plunged each sample, hissing
into liquid nitrogen or left it resting on
a glacier of dry ice.

So the individuals were saved,
to travel later through a sieve, of sorts,
a screen to spot just where each
was damaged, map a certain tweak
to a specific freak, reconciling inner-scape
with outer trait.

POOL

Clear, chlorine-scented water-box, tall,
tiled room. Torpedo-
headed swimmers pull themselves
down lanes and back.

Perched on the observation
    deck, I'd watch them practice after my own
    swim. Each water-gait. Does it descend
    from each own angle, strength, flex?

From a learned idea? See that flailing one,
    fast enough, but what cost the gesture, saying
    my shoulders are of steel.

        And there again: the man I saw and swam
beside, and sometimes watched, arms the same, cutting through
the pool,
a smooth machine
leaving and leaving again, nothing
behind him in the water
but a swirl. A question mark
forming and reforming.

JELLYFISH

What cleanly-drawn, transparent beings,
lit, encased for education's sake
in fluid neither flown nor flowing:

your umbilically corded brain's
a ring, your world's the same

on every side. Handless, eyeless,
what have you to say to those of us with faces,
who have faced and turned, and turned,

and piled our ghostly fingers
on your glass?

*Nothing at all—a lung,
a flutter, not a thing—
the thin
difference between
pushing away and letting in.*

INDIVIDUALS

Some trickled to the coast
from sage or forest,
others from the cool
suburban rain.
Loosed on the city,
we worked where
they would have us,
coasted through the pinkish hour
before the early shift,
drank porters, ales, mojitos,
sangrias, sours
from jars or glasses
cans or bottles or
whatever was at hand,
gathered in classrooms, houses
porches, parks, apartments,
collected shoes
and parking tickets,
tangled with each other,
danced together,
found motifs
and closed our eyes
and slept.

Ours was the dizzy
of samaras. The sky

was an oyster shell
that sometimes cracked.
We were afflicted with
the itch of winged fruit
made to spin
find ground
break open
and take root.

INDOCTRINATION

By measures I
was let into the lab,
its islands of black benchtop,
shelves bejeweled with motley flasks.
It harbored busy strangers
who did not look up.

By measures: *isolate
and quantify* the DNA from our library
of leaf-bits sampled
from the greenhouse occupants.

P narrated and performed the task:
the cell walls broken by brute violence,
the tightly coiled DNA coaxed apart by heat,
the helix held by cold and chloroform and salts.
The fume hood hummed; the centrifuge
spun macerated pulp to the bottom of the tube.
P drew an emerald fluid
off the top, then added alcohol,
arctic and familiar.
Forced out of solution, our molecule
precipitated, floated down
in flakes.

For my purposes, the story mattered less
than the best way to array reagents in the hood

unscrew each bottle cap so *DNAses*
didn't wander in on motes,
—minute details.
All this I learned, and how to hold the mortar
as I ground the leaves so none escaped.

Terse tips leapt
from P and the others.
How not to trust the instruments
("because the dial *says*
thirty-seven doesn't mean it *is!*")
to speak precisely ("was it *like*
or *was* it?"), to speak
as they all did (spin down, ramp up,
titrate, dilute, inoculate, pour a gel,
run it again, and again). How to pass
one's senses through one's mind,
how to remove oneself.

Compounds of common use.
How cold can rescue anything alive
from chaos. So many kinds of frozen;
all that ice crystals destroy in their
advance.

A small world loomed, a forest
of forces. At home M watched me watch
the cream exploding
in my coffee cup.

IN ABSOLUTES
WE SEEK EACH OTHER

Each of us had sheets
of music, M and I,
in stacks somewhere—vestiges of a shared
evolutionary phase. A neighbor whom we never saw
blew trumpet scales into the air on sunny days
and M—the better student—
called the keys.

Afternoons I walked under a rush of trees.
Wind visited the hillside before a cold diurnal rain
and overturned the silver side of leaves,
and shivered all of them at once, together.

HATCHERY

Whatever you are
you are blue at
the fringes. You
wear the
cartoonish color
of cold.

Whatever you *are*,

sum of roe
and milk,

your blunted
noses align toward
me.

Whatever I am
here you come,

a one-brained riot,
an onslaught
of famished raindrops.

*

On the barn's wide roof,
one shingle-clone.

One bred rose
in a long, long hedge…

I track one Coho
in the tank

as if there could exist a further fact

behind her ball-peen nose
her cold electric skin

her complexion a sky
in mixed weather.

I want there to be something
single in her swim

a self in the planned
body.

I hold her in my eye.
There, and there, and then—

but she is gone
in the sibling-hover.

BODIES IN MOTION

The bar: a wall
of windows, blue
Christmas lights all year,
waitress a lovely sylph.
Everyone we knew and half-knew
passing one the street.

The swimmer, across the table,
sipped cheap Scotch, saying things
I thought I was alone
in thinking…

The ceiling was all mirrors.
Glancing up, I'd note our
position, me here, him there,
bodies periodically carried back to this
eclipse. That night or the next he'd veer off into dark
then disappear, and disappear, and disappear.

THE ISOLATE

Re-suspended,
DNA could pass
for water, a liquid
blip in a clear plastic tube.

So clean,
a being's extract,
singular, seething almost:
information, to be
read.

The plant, long since
compost, was code
made manifest
in cyclic marches
code itself set off—thus matter
begat matter, so its leaves unhid…

One tube resting
in one row of one blue plastic rack
held one plant's
isolate. I'd have rows
and rows, and racks. When I worked alone
I'd wander sometimes to the window
and look out.

POSSESSIONS

We had the small, unfinished table Rachel left.
Our mauve-splotched plates were from M's mom's garage.
We had a pantry full of Goodwill mason jars.
M found our bookshelves on the sidewalk coming home.

Sometimes it seemed we had a hundred days of rain,
rain on liquid windows, a ceiling stained with damp.
On Saturday we had KCMU or Aimee Mann and hours
of robes and tea and talk. M eventually

had someplace to go. Most nights I had no firm plans.
I had the radio: *The Swing Years* with Cynthia Doyon,
whose voice was tarnished silver, whose body would be found
—floating, head-shot, with a note—right by the lab.

I had my eyes closed, lying on the bed, rewinding
recent appearances of the swimming man,
his form appearing from the campus crowd.
His white shirt, hair gleaming wet, shoulders set

like no one else's, quite.

IN SITU

At home.
Green room, mattresses
stacked, green sheets. No bed.
Desk of sorts.
Window blinding bright—
Yes, I remember:
afternoon light rippling
the ceiling as if it were
a boat's white metal
pockmarked prow slapping
waves, as if the house
were moving.

Downstairs the neighbor's cats
flickering, M's singing
in the stairs…

A chromosome: miles of code
wound up into X,
mysterious. We get
to know it with a fluorescent
bit of sequence, a probe
that homes
to its corresponding place
in the chromosome's
dark landscape,
or does not. We know the chromosome
by what knows it.

The constituent's revealed
by the logic of a match
the bloom by its bee, the tree
by its bird, the pen
by the hand holding it
and writing.

GELS

There was a thrill in learning the tricks,
the instruments to trade for an eye.

Compound that would cling to the rungs
of a helix and fluoresce in UV light

Gels, acrylamide or agarose:
matrices in which mysterious isolates were measured,
unknowns compared with knowns,
as swimmers separate, are measured in
the medium of *pool*.

You'd bend to drop the isolate (dyed blue, so you
could see it) into a well, a tiny, perfect notch
in the clean, firm field;

connect the electrodes,
flick the switch to on,
your sample with its small minus charge migrating
down the gel, pulled slowly through the matrix toward
the bigger plus, the whole rig
warm and bubbling.

¤

Here is what happens: the lab coat
becomes you, as your vanishing act
improves: in the darkroom, hit

the ultraviolet, the ethidium-tagged fragment
springs, fluorescent, into focus
as your skin disappears under blacklight.

POOL

The pool and I reach equilibrium, as a person
numbs to wind, gets used to it, this hard
contending with a stretch
of time and space, as quick-caught breaths add up
to lengths and laps.

Levered back to land, the body
knows itself again
as *tired, all places
tried…*

How do we get anywhere?
What's past re-members
what is next: the hand, plunged in,
creates the micro-current I will swim
against, as the prevailing vision
rises up before our eyes
to meet the hours halfway.

SEARCH ENGINE

Wake and stumble to the screen,
see what's gone wrong. White dawn
fills drawn shades:
day's indicator light,
switched on. Me blinking,

    (search weather portland or)

wires not touching, something

    (search weather san diego ca)

not touching.

    (search sand)
    Me reading

    (search history sand)

history of the sand
mandala, the Navajo sand painting,
the Roman arena, miles from sand,
in my head rehearsing
the walk to the car,

(search recipe beets)

the trip
the hum, the wet, unclimb-able

(search linden trees)

not-linden trees
the stumble to the desk
to see what's gone wrong: untouched, touching
nothing but keys and dust.

¤

A population flows
across this field where I used
to try to see the swimmer after class—
each destined in a group or pair
or by himself, and it is not him

walking across the grass, it
is not him with his shoulders fixed
and heading for the pool, it is
not him with his downward gaze, not
him, but something in my eye.

2

COORDINATES

DRIVING NORTH

The dark started as blue around
the edge of things; trees along the road
grew strange; shadows drowned the page
you were reading. Now, as the final ferry
turns north, the rusted hull sounds hollow in
the waves. Islanders visit in the deck's green light,
leaning into each other's windows. I point out the blacksmith
with his sea-licked curls; I whisper you the story
of his previous life…

I'm from here: I know I'll need a pair of boots.
That some days the sun will be a projectionist's bulb
and we'll be actors on a flat-lit screen.
That we'll step into nights so dark I could be
touching your sleeve, and not see you.

BARNACLES

Witness them swimming,
thinking of swimming.
The mother: precedent.
The daughter: unimproved.
See them balanced on fleshpins
in an amphitheater of sandstone.
A barge disturbs their blinding mirror.
The sea, the rich surround, by
wavelets comes.

You, tiny onlookers,
are now and ever home.
Both oculus and dome.
Sharp, silent citizens.

ANATOMY

Behind the eyelid: copper sky

The open palm: a web

The collarbone: a crested wave

(A thousand waves, then bed)

The risen knee: cathedral dome

Beneath the shirtsleeve: white

The spine at rest: suspension bridge

The lucky lung: a kite

SAVANTS

The same-faced houses are waiting for the sea.
Their ledges keep binoculars, their walls
hang maps of depths. In bedrooms made
to harbor light, the children wake.

Fathers slouch in patio chairs, glancing
from their sun hats toward contingent things:
a sail snapped full, a gull hanging on air,
answering each wrinkle in the wind.

The children have absorbed
more knowledge than you'd guess: the logic
of the lens, the evolution of the wing. They've seen
in time-lapse video, the blind, dynamic earth……

Tonight, before sleeping, they'll conjure the trip
over contour lines to the blistering deep,
the sonar's ping, the drop-off place,
where the seafloor departs from the map.

APERTURES

The herring had just run down the coast.
Their pearled roe clung to every nook and weed.
A frenzy of birds descended in their wake.
And following the birds, sea lions in heat, their song
across the water like a string bowed to tearing.
We too were drawn to the water's edge,
where the sea grew into all the rocks' depressions.
You peered into tide pools. I stumbled with my camera,
deciding how much to let in. Keep the shade that let
me see, one tiny pinhole against all this light, remain
unmoved? Or dial the aperture wide, and risk
the picture: join the mingling we were meant for.
In love, turn permeable, like the clouds in the southward sky
streaking up and up like the handwriting of an ecstatic.

BLOOD HARMONY

We pulled the glass-green bottles
from the shipwreck for their strangeness: that gray

a green, that curve, that shape of lip. August,
we stop noticing the crickets,

the furious vibrations in the grass. And when
we're gathered at the long, plank table

and wind turns toward us, we forget
the fixed, blind bottles, their open throats, the sound

of empty vessels calling to their kind. How wave
breaking on black rock consigns to wave.

MOON SNAIL

Even the moon has its own snail,
gnomic, removed
under miles of water, its pale
foot reaching for a shape to hold.
In mornings the light stretched
in cold arcs across the parking lot.
Inside, we circled: table to kitchen to mirror.
Decided we could go into town or not.
The shore's too many rounded rocks,
exotic jade and red, all dried to gray in my hand,
then lay on the white plastic table next to yours.
The pieces of the world are calling
to each other: you were looking
for the moon snail's husk, a fist-sized
echo, washed into sight.

ANATOMY

The ruffled heart: a sea

The iris-flinch: anemone

Counterbalanced ribs: give way

Between the hips: the drifted snow

The thumbnail: dawn

The neck: bastille

The fingertips: foment unrest

The risen vein: a rope across

an awkward load: the fist

COORDINATES

The night is glass, is dark unshattered glass.
I drive her home and learn how much she's lost.
She's forgotten my mother, whom she saw minutes before.
We're floating in my mother's quiet car.

She's forgotten what to be unkind about.
Her horns are blunted, fangs worn down.
She's a grass-fed creature nosing in the grass.
Her baseless pleasantries meet my dishonest own.

Children trickle from the beach at dusk
with golden, graven backs, bare high-held feet.
Every stone's the same, but I'm a clothed adult.
A stranger on the road at an odd hour.

I pass with care and leave her where she lives.
The station takes me back through darker air.
*…one-two-four-point-five degrees…Jericho
winds Southeast three-zero gusting to three-five…*

*Chrome Island, seas two-foot chop…*and so on.
From points, a picture: we're in the calmest seas.
I know that I should stay here living in the weather
the way I know that house aglow behind the cedar.

Later, on the deck, eyes closed, it is the same.
Bottle clinked on pile, brushed branch, retreating car.
The night sounds crack a fissure in my shore.
The night unfolds inside me like a vast black net

and all that moves inside it—the owl alight
inside it—reaches me and tells me where I am.

TELEOLOGY OF ISLANDS

What is there to say, night swimmer,
lodged in the kindled mechanism of the stars,
black water pooling around your feet.
The curved arms of the white plastic chair
you dragged from someone's summer house
draw the colder pieces of light.
Breath wells up, overflowing the ribs,
as blood brings heat to every restless cell,
where your lonely genes are coiling
and uncoiling in the dark, as the droplets dry
to crystal on your skin, as your body goes on
expressing what it can. As the beacon
sweeps around again, catching the cedars
and madrones across the bay, throwing
prehistoric shadows on the black, unfinished coast.

WHITE

Behind a sign, behind a
script, the blank, before.

A long Antarctica of hotel sheets.
Away, I could be anyone.

But closer, the cloud bank's light-bloom,
the snowfield's drone.
The empty-never-empty.
A whiteout, a swarm.

The freeway we no longer hear, the sound
no story rises from.

The underlying: breakfast over, dishes done,
and put away, and you
are here, and here

you are. The underlying: I've touched
you again, before knowing
I wanted to touch you.

ANATOMY

Head: a midday cinema

Down arms: warm thunder rolls

Drops: a souvenir

of sea: that country never yours

Risen skin: a prickled field

Throat: an empty door

Breath: the shorebirds swoop and sail

Blood: the sea's echo

AUBADE

The island's close-up skin
fills the windshield: cliff-side pines
morning blue in two dimensions.
As the ferry mumbles into gear and pulls
us back, detail disperses into blur,
the shape of it now visible—

where we lapsed, intertidal.
Where you loomed, hauling back against
the oars, big in the poster-size frame
of memory, my leg in the foreground
slung over the gunnel, toes in
the fine, cold, finite sea…

The ferry swings us round to face another shore.
The island's black profile slides left.
And so we part. It stays put. We're taken up
by freeways, whisked to bigger ferries,
finally pumped into the mainland, all of us
by the mile getting smaller.

ARC & CHORD

The geese would have been high, white specks
on a blank sky until you found the voice to call them in.
You hailed and hailed while your brothers traced
the arc of their descent and dropped them to the lake.
The dogs wrestled the heaving bodies
back to you, their black eyes vitrified by then,
as the circle closed, and a mound of snow geese
grew around your feet. Now, when night
is creeping up the walls, when winter
is opening its throat around this place, there's nothing—
not your jacket, not your inlaid knife—
that will tell me what it's like to turn the flock,
to call and get the answer.

for my father

MEANWHILE

Dare you go into a world of rain, you'll
pick your way along a face of black basalt
discussing other people's problems.
Conversation will circle back to trouble—
failed partnerships, economies, the afternoon
the young, rich girlfriend of a friend
was found to be untrue.
Meanwhile, the rain will pierce
your tightest weave; grape-size drops
will splatter on your nose.
I'm talking *rain*: an instrument
re-sketching every place you thought you knew,
finding rivulets in rock, pooling in
your pack, crumbling roads you never thought
to think about, making the creek
below into a wide white beast,
turning babble upon babble into roar.

PROLOGUE

Pregnant, dreaming, I hold a fish
an animated muscle, a tangle-brain.
I bend amid a stream and feel
below the fanning gills
its perfect, twitching flesh…
and wake
and roll back into sleep—
a cell culture dish: something
in me growing and awake.

ACKNOWLEDGMENTS

Poems in this collection first appeared in the following journals, sometimes in different versions:

Burnside Review ("White")
The Cortland Review (the first "Anatomy")
Mid-American Review ("Blood Harmony," "Arc & Chord")
The New Republic ("Apertures")
Prairie Schooner ("Jellyfish," "Savants," and "Teleology of Islands")
The Paris Review ("Moon Snail")
Red Rock Review ("Driving North")
Subtropics ("Barnacles")
Tin House (the second "Anatomy")
Verse Daily ("White")

Thanks to Literary Arts for fellowship support and to Meredith Cole, Megan Snyder-Camp, and Carl Adamschick for readings and advice. Thanks especially to Kevin Edwards for insight and encouragement.

JESSICA JOHNSON was raised in the rural West and educated in poetry and biology at the University of Washington. She teaches at Portland Community College.

❧

COLOPHON

Text is set in a digital version of Jenson, designed by Robert Slimbach in 1996, and based on the work of punchcutter, printer, and publisher Nicolas Jenson. The titles are in Futura.

NEW MICHIGAN PRESS, based in Tucson, Arizona, prints poetry and prose chapbooks, especially work that transcends traditional genre. Together with DIAGRAM, NMP sponsors a yearly chapbook competition. Jessica won the 2014 competition.

DIAGRAM, a journal of text, art, and schematic, is published bimonthly at THEDIAGRAM.COM. Periodic print anthologies are available from the New Michigan Press at NEWMICHIGANPRESS.COM/NMP.

www.ingramcontent.com/pod-product-compliance
Lightning Source LLC
Chambersburg PA
CBHW031503040426
42444CB00007B/1190